Magic, Myth, and Mystery

KRAMPUS

DO YOU BELIEVE?

This series features creatures that excite our minds. They're magical. They're mythical. They're mysterious. They're also not real. They live in our stories. They're brought to life by our imaginations. Facts about these creatures are based on folklore, legends, and beliefs. We have a rich history of believing in the impossible. But these creatures only live in fantasies and dreams. Monsters do not live under our beds. They live in our heads!

45th Parallel Press

Published in the United States of America by Cherry Lake Publishing
Ann Arbor, Michigan
www.cherrylakepublishing.com

Reading Adviser: Marla Conn MS, Ed., Literacy specialist, Read-Ability, Inc.
Book Design: Felicia Macheske

Photo Credits: © © najin/iStock.com, cover; © BeSilvestre/Shutterstock.com, cover; © My name is boy/Shutterstock.com, cover; © poidl/Shutterstock.com, 1, 7; © Volodymyr Tverdokhlib/Shutterstock.com, 5; © Directornico/Shutterstock.com, 8; © dmitry_7/iStock.com, 11; © Lordn/Shutterstock.com, 13; © Kamira/Shutterstock.com, 15; © eldar nurkovic/Shutterstock.com, 16; © FooTToo/Shutterstock.com, 19; © sergo1972/Shutterstock.com, 20; © Kiselev Andrey Valerevich/Shutterstock.com, 22; © Mark Time Author/Shutterstock.com, 25; © Alina Reviakina/Shutterstock.com, 27; © Jonah_H/Shutterstock.com, 28

Graphic Elements Throughout: © denniro/Shutterstock.com; © Libellule/Shutterstock.com; © sociologas/Shutterstock.com; © paprika/Shutterstock.com; © ilolab/Shutterstock.com; © Bruce Rolff/Shutterstock.com

45th Parallel Press is an imprint of Cherry Lake Publishing.

Library of Congress Cataloging-in-Publication Data has been filed and is available at catalog.loc.gov

Cherry Lake Publishing would like to acknowledge the work of The Partnership for 21st Century Skills. Please visit *www.p21.org* for more information.

Printed in the United States of America
Corporate Graphics Inc.

TABLE of CONTENTS

Chapter One
Krampus Is Coming to Town! ... 4

Chapter Two
You Better Watch Out! ... 10

Chapter Three
Cramping Krampus's Style ... 14

Chapter Four
From Hel and Back ... 18

Chapter Five
Krampus and Company ... 24

Did You Know? ... 30
Consider This! ... 31
Learn More ... 31
Glossary ... 32
Index ... 32
About the Author ... 32

Chapter One

Krampus Is Coming to Town!

What does Krampus look like? What is Krampus Night? What is Krampus Run?

"Have you been **naughty** or nice?" Naughty means bad. Krampus is a Christmas monster. He punishes naughty children.

Krampus is half-goat. He's half-**demon**. Demons are monsters. Krampus has goat horns. The horns are sharp. They curl up. Krampus is ugly. He has a long face. He has a beard. He's hairy. He has black fur. He has a long, pointed tongue. He has fangs.

He has red, bloody eyes. He has a long tail. He has sharp claws. He has **cloven hooves**. Cloven means split. Hooves are hard coverings of animal feet.

Krampus carries chains. He wears cowbells. He carries bundles of sticks. Sometimes, he carries a whip. He carries a basket. The basket is strapped to his back.

Krampus's tongue sticks out of his mouth.

Explained by Science!

Krampus has cloven hooves. Goats have cloven hooves. Other animals with cloven hooves are cows, deer, and sheep. This means the hooves are split into two toes. These two toes are like a human's third and fourth fingers. They're like claws. The space between the claws is called the interdigital cleft. The skin is called the interdigital skin. The skin is like soft pads. The covering of the hoof is called the horn. It's hard. It's like human fingernails. Cloven hooves let animals move on tough land. They have good grip. This lets animals climb steep mountains. They do this to find food. Cloven hooves help animals survive.

Krampus lives in caves in the Alps.

Krampus comes in December. He comes the night before the **Feast** of Saint Nicholas. Feasts are parties with food. Saint Nicholas was a famous man. He gave away presents. He inspired Santa Claus stories.

The Feast of Saint Nicholas is celebrated in Europe. It's celebrated on December 6. Krampus Night is December 5. Krampus walks the streets. He visits homes. He punishes bad children.

On Krampus Night, German children are really good. They don't want to make Krampus mad. They want to live through the night. Good children get a gift on December 6.

Krampus Run is an old tradition. Young men would dress up. They wore fur suits. They wore wooden masks. They carried cowbells. They walked through town. They did this to get rid of winter's ghosts.

Today, people celebrate Krampus Night. They make it a party. They dress up like Krampus. They wear wooden masks. The masks look like Krampus. People wear bells. They wear chains. They do a Krampus Run. They run through town. They scare people. They chase people. They hit them with sticks or whips. They aim for people's legs. It's a crazy time!

There are Krampus balls.
Balls are dances.

Chapter Two

You Better Watch Out!

What does Krampus do? How does he work with Santa?

Krampus travels with Santa. Some say he's Santa's enemy. Some say he's Santa's partner. He deals with naughty children. Santa deals with nice children. Krampus warns people he's coming. His cloven hooves make loud clicks. He rings his cowbells. He shakes his chains. Chains mean he's bound to the devil.

On Krampus Night, children put out their shoes. Good children get a present. They get it from Santa.

Bad children get coal or twigs. They get it from Krampus. Parents take the twigs. They hang them on the wall. This reminds children to be good.

Krampus carries a bag of birch sticks. He uses them to whip bad children.

When Fantasy Meets Reality!

A baby goat was born. It looked like a demon. This happened in San Luis. San Luis is in central Argentina. The baby goat was deformed. Deformed means not normal. The baby goat had eyes that stuck out. It had a flat face. Its face looked like a human. The rest of the body was normal. It only lived for 3 hours. Everyone was shocked. The goat belonged to Gladys Oveido. Oveido was confused. She found it in the family's field. The baby goat's mother had two other kids. Kids are baby goats. Oveido tried to feed the baby goat. She gave it milk from a spoon. She said, "She began to fail her breathing. And after a while, she died." Oveido's daughter-in-law took pictures. She shared them online. Many people saw the pictures.

Krampus also attacks young lovers.

People think Krampus kidnaps really bad children. He goes to their houses. He whips them. He beats them. He pulls their hair. He pulls their ears. He puts children in his basket. He carries them away.

Some stories say he does different things to the children. He cooks them. He eats them. He takes them to the underworld. He leads them off cliffs. He has them live with him for a year. He treats them like slaves.

Krampus is strong. He's scary. People believe he scares kids into behaving. He feeds off children's fears. He knows when children are bad. Good children don't have to worry. They're safe. Krampus is fair. He won't harm good children.

Chapter Three

Cramping Krampus's Style

How do parents use Krampus? What are ways to protect against Krampus?

Parents use Krampus as a warning. They want children to be good. They use Krampus to scare children. They say things like, "Behave, or Krampus will get you."

Some parents help Krampus. They want Krampus to punish their children. They use chalk. They draw a special sign. They do this above the front door. They do this on Krampus Night. They welcome Krampus inside the house.

Children can fight back. They can erase the sign. This lessens the chance of Krampus coming. But he can still come. Drawing the sign alerts him.

Some stories say Krampus can't enter a house unless he's invited.

Churches use signs to help fight demons.

Children can get even with their parents. They draw the sign again. They draw it upside down. They draw it backward. This turns Krampus against those who drew the sign in the first place.

Some stories say giving Krampus a gift will stop him. Children can give Krampus fruit. Krampus likes apples and oranges. He'll sit down to eat the fruit. He'll share it. He'll leave.

Krampus is **immortal**. Immortal means living forever. He can be killed. But he will return each December.

SURVIVAL TIPS!

- Be good. Stay out of trouble. This is the only way to avoid Krampus.
- Stay alert. Be aware of everything around you.
- Don't take pictures of Krampus. This annoys Krampus. Don't make him mad. Don't take selfies with him.
- Don't make eye contact. This means you want to fight.
- Don't tease Krampus. He doesn't have a sense of humor.
- Wear pads on your body. Wear shin guards. Protect yourself from getting whipped.
- Hide in a tight space. Krampus is big. It's hard for him to get into small areas.
- Stay awake. Don't sleep. Be ready!

Chapter Four

From Hel and Back

Who is Hel? What is the Yule Goat? Who is the Horned God? Who is Pan?

Krampus's name comes from krampen. Krampen is a German word. It means "claw." Krampus has sharp, scary claws. He also grabs children. So his name makes sense.

Some people think Krampus is Hel's son. Hel is a **Norse** goddess. Norse refers to the area around Norway. Norse people were Vikings. Hel is the goddess of the **underworld**. The underworld is hell.

It's where the dead live. Some people think Krampus drags children to hell. He brings bad children to his mother.

Krampus is popular in areas around Germany, Austria, and Norway.

Some people think Krampus is related to the **Yule** Goat. Yule means Christmas. The Yule Goat is a Norse character. It scared children. It made children honor Christmas traditions.

Christianity is a religion. Christians honored Old Man Winter and Saint Nicholas. The Christmas holiday became popular. Stories about Santa Claus were told. People also told stories about **anti-**Santa. Anti means opposite. The Yule Goat became Krampus. Krampus was like the Christians' devil. It makes sense to have Krampus be a Christmas monster. Krampus was most active during long nights. This happens around **Yuletide**. Yuletide is Christmastime. It's in December.

In some stories, Krampus and Santa work together.

Some people think Krampus is related to the Horned God. The Horned God is part of **Wicca**. Wicca is like a religion. It's connected to witches and magic. The Horned God is the energy in animals and the wild. He has horns. He's the union of the **divine** and animals. Divine means god-like. The Horned God carries dead people's souls to the underworld.

Some people think Krampus is related to Pan. Pan is a Greek god. He's the god of nature and music. He has goat horns. He has goat legs. He has cloven hooves.

Krampus balances good with evil.

Know the Lingo!*

*Krampus lingo words are German in origin

- **Brav Sein:** Be good!
- **Butte:** child-sized basket or tub carried on Krampus's back
- **Geschenk:** present, gift
- **Heiligabend:** Christmas Eve
- **Krampen:** claw
- **Krampusgruppe:** group of people who celebrate Krampus Night
- **Krampuslauf:** Krampus Run
- **Krampusnacht:** Krampus Night
- **Krampusse:** more than one person dressed up like Krampus
- **Larven:** Krampus costumes that include sheep's skin, horns, and wooden masks
- **Reizen:** to tease
- **Rute:** rod
- **Teufel:** the devil
- **Tratzen:** to tease
- **Weidenruten:** bundles of birch sticks
- **Weihnachten:** Christmas
- **Winterzeit:** winter

Chapter Five

Krampus and Company

Who is Hans Trapp? Who is Father Whipper? Who is Knecht Ruprecht?

Krampus isn't the only anti-Santa. There are others.

Hans Trapp is from France. He was rich. He was greedy. He wanted all the lands around him. He made a deal with the devil. The Church found out. They kicked him out. Trapp was sent to the forest. He became crazy. He dressed up as a scarecrow. He came out at Christmas. He scared children. He kidnapped bad children. He ate them. Then, lightning hit him. He was killed.

But parents still yell, “Hans Trapp is coming! Hans Trapp is coming!”

Trapp was based on a real man named Hans von Trotha.

Real-World Connection

Krampus isn't the only goat-man. Thomas Thwaites became a goat. He wrote a book. The book is called *GoatMan: How I Took a Holiday from Being Human*. He acted like a goat for 3 days. He wore a goat suit. He walked on his hands. He hung out in a goat herd. He grazed. He ate grass. He sniffed at other goats. He hung out with a goat-friend. He slept outside. He climbed steep cliffs. He did this in the Swiss Alps. Why did he do this? He owed money. He lived with his father. He couldn't find a job. He worried a lot. He wanted to escape his life. He wanted to see things from an animal's perspective. First, he wanted to become an elephant. But someone told him he was closer to a goat. So, he became a goat.

Father Whipper is another anti-Santa. He's from France. He wears a dark fur coat. He has a long beard. He was an evil **butcher**. Butchers are people who cut and sell meat. Father Whipper ate three boys. Santa saved them. He brought the children back to life. He **enslaved** Father Whipper. Enslave means to make someone a slave. Father Whipper works for Santa. He punishes bad children. He beats them. He uses a whip. He leaves them coal.

Father Whipper is also known as Père Fouettard.

Knecht Ruprecht is another anti-Santa. He wears fur coats. He wears a pointed hood. He limps. He uses a long cane. He carries a bag of ashes. He wears little bells.

He asks children if they pray. If children pray, Ruprecht gives them treats from Santa. If they don't, he hits them with his bag. He leaves them stones, coal, or sticks. The sticks are for parents to spank their children.

Knecht Ruprecht is more famous than Krampus. But Krampus is much scarier. Be good, for goodness' sake!

Ruprecht was an orphan. Santa raised him.

Did You Know?

- In the 1930s, Austria was under Fascist rule. Fascism means one leader controls everything. Krampus was seen as a sin. People couldn't celebrate Krampus Night. People dressed as Krampus were taken to jail.
- Ludwig Schnegg is a carver. He makes Krampus masks. He's been doing this since 1981. He makes masks for all 80 members of a Krampus group.
- There are two towns in Austria. The towns are Kitzbühel and Stallhofen. They have Krampus museums. The museums collect costumes. They collect masks.
- Krampus celebrations are starting to be popular in the United States. Los Angeles, California, hosts Krampus events. A museum in Brooklyn, New York, hosts Krampus costume parties.
- Europeans give Krampus greeting cards. They've been doing this since the 1800s. They're called Krampuskarten. The cards read, "Gruss vom Krampus!" This means "Greetings from Krampus!" The cards have funny rhymes.
- In Croatia, Krampus is a devil. He wears a cloth sack around his waist. He wears chains. Santa gave golden sticks to good children. Bad children saw their gifts taken away by Krampus. He left silver instead.

Consider This!

Take a Position: What do you think about Krampus Night? Some people think it's too dangerous. Some people think it's too scary. Some think it should be banned. This means we shouldn't celebrate it anymore. Do you think it should be banned? Argue your point with reasons and evidence.

Say What? Compare Santa Claus and Krampus. Explain how they are the same. Explain how they are different. Which one do you think is more interesting?

Think About It! Some think Krampus is the anti-hero of Santa Claus. Anti-heroes are the opposite of heroes. The hero is good. The anti-hero is bad. Think of other heroes and anti-heroes. Make a list. Then, create your own hero. Create your own anti-hero.

Learn More

- Beauchamp, Monte. *Krampus: The Devil of Christmas*. San Francisco: Last Gasp, 2010.
- Dougherty, Michael. *Krampus: Shadow of Saint Nicholas*. Burbank, CA: Legendary Comics, 2015.

Glossary

anti- (AN-tye) against or opposite

butcher (BUCH-ur) person who cuts and sells meat

Christianity (kris-chee-AN-ih-tee) a specific religion

cloven (KLOVE-in) split

demon (DEE-muhn) evil monster

divine (dih-VINE) god-like

enslaved (en-SLAYVD) made someone a slave

feast (FEEST) party with food

hooves (HOOVZ) hard coverings of animal feet

immortal (ih-MOR-tuhl) living forever

naughty (NAW-tee) bad

Norse (NORS) from the Norway area, Vikings

underworld (UHN-dur-wurld) hell

Wicca (WIH-kuh) a pagan religion practiced by witches and involving folk magic

Yule (YOOL) Christmas

Yuletide (YOOL-tide) Christmastime

Index

anti-Santa, 21, 24–29
Christmas, 4, 21, 24, 30
Hel, 18–19
Horned God, 22
Krampus, 30
  and bad children, 10, 11, 13
  how parents use him, 14–15
  how to stop him, 16
  relatives, 18–22
  traditions, 9, 10
  what he does, 7, 10–13
  what he looks like, 4–5, 18
  where he lives, 6
lingo, 23
Pan, 22
Santa, 7, 10, 20, 21, 29
survival tips, 17
Yule Goat, 21

About the Author

Dr. Virginia Loh-Hagan is an author, university professor, former classroom teacher, and curriculum designer. She believes in Krampus! She tries to be nice all year long. She lives in San Diego, California, with her very tall husband and very naughty dogs.